Boost Your Insta Fame

\-

Complete Guide to Increase Followers on Instagram

I0422681

By Emanule Ascolillo
AgilMind

Sommario

Introduction

Welcome to the world of Instagram marketing, where building a successful online presence requires not only creativity and passion but also a deep understanding of the platform dynamics and the most effective strategies to achieve your goals. In this book, we will delve into the best practices and advanced techniques for increasing your Instagram profile followers and building an engaged and loyal community.

We will begin by thoroughly examining how Instagram's algorithm works and how it impacts the visibility of your content, then move on to discuss the importance of understanding your target audience and optimizing your Instagram profile to maximize attractiveness. Subsequently, we will explore creating engaging and high-quality content, strategic hashtag usage, and leveraging collaborations and partnerships to boost your profile visibility.

We will continue by analyzing how to use Instagram Stories to engage your audience, the importance of interaction and engagement for your profile's success, and conducting in-depth result analysis to adapt and optimize your growth strategy. Finally, we will explore advanced techniques to further accelerate follower growth, providing you with tools and resources to stand out in Instagram's vast and competitive arena.

Regardless of your level of experience on Instagram, this book will offer you a comprehensive and practical guide to increase your profile followers and build a successful online presence on this increasingly important social platform. Get ready to dive into the fascinating and dynamic world of Instagram marketing and discover everything you need to achieve your growth and visibility goals.

*NOTES:*_____

_____

_____

_____

_____

_____

_____

_____

_____

_____

_____

_____

_____

_____

_____

_____

_____

_____

_____

_____

_____

_____

_____

_____

_____

_____

_____

_____

_____

_____

_____

Chapter 1 - Deciphering the Instagram Algorithm

In the vast universe of social media, Instagram stands out as one of the most popular and influential platforms of our time. With over a billion monthly active users, Instagram has evolved beyond just a photo and video-sharing app; it has become a means to connect, express, and build online communities. However, behind the user-friendly interface and endless content scrolling lies a technical aspect that plays a crucial role in determining a profile's success: the Instagram algorithm.

In this chapter, we will delve deep into the algorithm powering Instagram, analyzing its components, mechanisms, and implications for those seeking to increase their visibility and following on the platform. Through a combination of research, analysis, and practical experience, we will strive to shed light on one of the most enigmatic and often misunderstood aspects of Instagram: how the algorithm truly works and how we can leverage it to our advantage.

Understanding the Instagram Algorithm: A Journey into the Heart of the Platform

To fully grasp the Instagram algorithm, we must first examine its objectives and functions. At first glance, the algorithm may seem like a complex set of rules and parameters, but at its core lies a simple goal: to provide users with relevant and engaging content. However, the way the algorithm achieves this goal is much more intricate than one might think.

Content Relevance: The Key to Engagement

At the core of the Instagram algorithm is content relevance. In other words, the algorithm seeks to identify and show users content that is most likely to interest and engage them. But how does Instagram determine content relevance? One of the main metrics used by the algorithm is engagement, which includes likes, comments, shares, and saves.

Hashtags and Keywords: Hashtags and keywords play a fundamental role in helping Instagram understand the content of a photo or video. When relevant hashtags are included in a post's description, it increases the likelihood of the post being shown to users who follow those hashtags or are interested in related topics.

Previous Interactions: Instagram takes into account users' past interactions with certain accounts and types of content to determine content relevance. If a user has previously positively interacted with posts from a certain account or on a certain topic, it's more likely that similar content will be shown to that user.

Viewing Time: The amount of time users spend viewing a particular post is another important indicator of relevance. Instagram considers viewing time when determining which posts to show users and in what order.

The Crucial Role of Engagement

Engagement is another key factor in the Instagram algorithm. Instagram seeks to promote content that generates meaningful interactions among users, such as likes, comments, shares, and saves. This is because engagement is an indicator of interest and involvement from users, and Instagram aims to provide users with content that interests and engages them.

Likes and Comments: The number of likes and comments a post receives is an important engagement indicator. Instagram takes into account the number of likes and comments when determining the relevance and popularity of a post.

Shares and Saves: Shares and saves are signals of quality content and value to users. Instagram considers shares and saves when determining which posts to show users and in what order.

Posting Frequency: The frequency of posting new content plays an important role in overall profile engagement. Instagram favors accounts that regularly post quality content, as it indicates consistent commitment and genuine interest from the user in interacting with the platform.

Challenges and Opportunities: Navigating the Instagram Algorithm Maze

Navigating the complex ecosystem of the Instagram algorithm can be challenging, but it's also an opportunity for those willing to dedicate time, resources, and creativity to understand and fully leverage the platform's potential. In the upcoming chapters, we will explore in detail the most effective strategies and tactics for increasing followers on Instagram, taking into account the key factors influencing the algorithm. From profile optimization techniques to creating engaging content, we will discover together how to maximize Instagram's potential to build a successful online presence.

*NOTES:*_____

Chapter 2 - Understanding Your Target Audience

In the fast-paced world of social media, understanding your target audience is crucial for increasing follower count on Instagram. The more you know about your audience, the better you can create targeted content that attracts and engages desired users. In this chapter, we will explore different strategies and tools to analyze Instagram's audience to develop a better understanding of who your followers are and how you can best meet their needs and interests.

Introduction

When it comes to building a presence on Instagram, it's not just about gaining a large number of followers, but also about creating an engaged community interested in your content. This begins with a thorough understanding of your target audience.

Demographic Analysis

The first step in understanding your target audience on Instagram is analyzing their demographic characteristics. This includes age, gender, geographic location, and other relevant demographic data. Tools like Instagram Insights provide valuable insights into these metrics, enabling you to create more targeted content.

Interest Analysis

In addition to demographic information, it's important to understand your audience's interests and preferences. This can be done by observing which types of content receive the most interactions and engagement. For example, if you're a fitness enthusiast and notice that workout-related posts receive more likes and comments, you might deduce that your audience is interested in fitness and health.

Engagement and Feedback

Audience engagement is an important indicator of the effectiveness of your content. Monitor likes, comments, and shares closely to understand which types of posts generate the most interest. Additionally, actively seek feedback from your audience through polls, questions in stories, or simply responding to comments. This will not only help you better understand your audience but also demonstrate that you value their opinions and engagement.

Metric Analysis

In addition to the information provided by Instagram Insights, it's useful to use external analytics tools to gain a deeper understanding of your audience's behavior. This may include analyzing demographic and behavioral data provided by platforms like Google Analytics or third-party tools specialized in social media analysis.

Creating Personas

An effective technique for better understanding your audience is to create personas, or imaginary profiles of your ideal followers. These profiles include demographic information, interests, behaviors, and goals, allowing you to create more targeted and relevant content for different segments of your audience.

Testing and Optimization

Once you've gathered information about your target audience, it's important to continuously test different strategies and content to optimize engagement and follower growth. Use A/B testing to compare the performance of different post variants and closely monitor metrics to identify what works best with your audience.

Conclusion

Understanding your target audience is a continuous and evolving process. By using a combination of analytics tools, audience feedback, and empirical testing, you can develop a thorough understanding of who your Instagram followers are and how you can create content that engages and inspires them. This knowledge will not only help you increase your follower count but also build an authentic and engaged community around your profile.

*NOTES:*_____

_____

_____

_____

_____

_____

_____

_____

_____

_____

_____

_____

_____

_____

_____

_____

_____

_____

_____

_____

_____

_____

_____

_____

_____

_____

_____

_____

Chapter 3 - Optimizing Your Instagram Profile to Maximize Attractiveness

In the competitive world of social media, having an optimized Instagram profile is crucial to grab audience attention and maximize the attractiveness of your account. In this chapter, we'll explore the best practices and strategies to optimize your Instagram profile to impress visitors and increase follower engagement.

Introduction

A well-optimized Instagram profile is like an attractive shop window inviting visitors to come in and explore. It's the first point of contact with your audience, so it's important to ensure it's captivating and representative of your brand or personality.

Profile Picture

The profile picture is the first thing people see when they visit your profile, so make sure it's high quality and clearly represents your brand or personality. If you're a brand, use the company logo; if you're an individual, use a recognizable photo that represents you well.

Username and Name

Your username and profile name are important for being easily found by Instagram users. Ensure your username is clear and related to your brand or identity. The profile name can be different from your username and is another opportunity to include relevant keywords for your industry.

Bio

The bio is where you can give a brief description of yourself or your brand. Make the most of the 150 characters available to grab attention and communicate who you are and what you do. Use relevant keywords and include a direct link to your website or an important landing page.

Link in Bio

Since Instagram only allows one link in the bio, make sure to maximize it. You can use services like Linktree to create a landing page with multiple links, allowing your followers to easily access additional content, products, or promotions.

Story Highlights

Story highlights are a fantastic opportunity to showcase your best content and main categories. Organize them logically and regularly update the content to keep the profile fresh and interesting for visitors.

Quality Content

There's no substitute for high-quality content when it comes to attracting and engaging followers on Instagram. Make sure to post well-crafted photos and videos that are interesting, informative, or entertaining for your target audience.

Strategic Hashtags

Use hashtags strategically to increase the visibility of your posts and attract new followers. Choose hashtags relevant to your industry and target audience, avoiding ones that are too generic or saturated.

Collaborations and Tagging

Collaborating with other Instagram users and tagging them in your posts is a great way to expand your audience and gain additional visibility. Look for partners or influencers in your industry and work with them to create engaging and shareable content.

Performance Monitoring

Finally, it's important to regularly monitor the performance of your Instagram profile using tools like Instagram Insights or third-party analytics platforms. This will allow you to identify which types of content work best with your audience and adapt your strategy accordingly.

Conclusion

Optimizing your Instagram profile is an ongoing process that requires time, commitment, and experimentation. By following the best practices and strategies described in this chapter, you can maximize the attractiveness of your account and increase engagement from your followers, contributing to the success and growth of your presence on Instagram.

*NOTES:*_____

Chapter 4 - Creating Engaging and Quality Content

Introduction

Instagram has become one of the primary social media channels for sharing visual content and connecting with the audience. To succeed on this platform, it's essential to create engaging and quality content that captures users' attention and encourages them to interact with your profile. In this chapter, we'll explore strategies, techniques, and tools for creating effective content on Instagram that can generate engagement and growth for your account.

Knowing Your Audience

Before you start creating content on Instagram, it's crucial to understand who your target audience is. Analyze your existing followers to understand their interests, preferences, and the types of content they find most engaging. Use tools like Instagram Insights to get detailed demographic and behavioral information about your audience. This knowledge will help you create targeted content that resonates with your audience.

Defining Your Content Strategy

Once you understand your audience, develop a clear and well-defined content strategy for your Instagram account. Decide what types of content you want to share (e.g., photos, videos, stories, promotional posts, etc.) and what themes or topics you want to address. Ensure that your content strategy aligns with the values and goals of your brand or personality.

Creating Original and Authentic Content

The key to success on Instagram is to create original and authentic content that stands out from the crowd. Avoid simply replicating what others are doing and instead try to find your unique voice and distinctive style. Be genuine, transparent, and share content that reflects your personality or brand authentically.

Investing in Visual Quality

Instagram is a visual platform, so it's essential to invest in the quality of the images and videos you share. Use a good quality camera or a phone with a high-resolution camera to take sharp and well-composed photos. Pay attention to lighting, composition, and focus to ensure that your images are visually appealing.

Experimenting with Different Formats and Content

Don't limit yourself to just one type of content on Instagram; experiment with a variety of formats and content to keep your audience interested and engaged. In addition to traditional photos, try sharing videos, stories, carousels, IGTV, and more. Try to understand which formats work best with your audience and adjust your strategy accordingly.

Using Stories Creatively

Instagram Stories are a great way to share temporary and spontaneous content with your audience. Use stories to show behind-the-scenes of your brand, ask questions to your followers, share exclusive content, or launch polls and quizzes. Take advantage of the various features of stories, such as GIFs, filters, and interactive polls, to make your content even more engaging.

Engaging Your Audience

Engagement is crucial on Instagram, so actively encourage your followers to interact with your content. Ask them to comment, like, share, or save your posts, and always respond to comments and direct messages to keep the dialogue with your audience. Also, organize contests or giveaways to stimulate interaction and participation.

Using Hashtags Strategically

Hashtags are a powerful tool to increase the visibility of your content on Instagram. Use relevant hashtags that are pertinent to your content and your target audience, but avoid using hashtags that are too generic or saturated. Also, create customized hashtags for your brand or specific campaigns and encourage your followers to use them in their posts.

Monitoring and Analyzing Hashtag Performance

Once you've started using hashtags in your posts, it's essential to monitor and analyze their performance to understand which ones are most effective for your audience. Use analytics tools like Instagram Insights, TikTok Analytics, or Twitter Analytics to monitor reach, impression, and engagement generated by each hashtag. Based on this data, you can optimize your hashtag strategy and focus on those that generate the best results.

Adapting Your Hashtag Strategy

Finally, remember that the hashtag strategy is not static and should be continuously adapted and optimized based on changes in your audience, social media algorithms, and market trends. Experiment with new hashtags, monitor the results, and make any changes to your hashtag strategy based on feedback and results obtained.

Conclusion

Using hashtags strategically is essential to increase the visibility, engagement, and success of your content on social media. Follow the best practices and strategies described in this chapter to select the most relevant and effective hashtags for your target audience and to optimize your content strategy on platforms like Instagram, TikTok, and Twitter. Experiment, monitor the results, and adapt your hashtag strategy based on feedback and results obtained, and you'll see your presence and influence on social media grow.

*NOTES:*_____

_____

_____

_____

_____

_____

_____

_____

_____

_____

_____

_____

_____

_____

_____

_____

_____

_____

_____

_____

_____

_____

_____

_____

_____

_____

_____

_____

Chapter 5 - Using Hashtags Strategically

Introduction

Hashtags have become a fundamental tool for increasing content visibility on social platforms like Instagram, Twitter, and TikTok. When used strategically, hashtags can help you reach a wider audience, increase engagement, and build an active community around your profile. In this chapter, we'll explore best practices and strategies for using hashtags effectively and achieving optimal results.

Understanding the Power of Hashtags

Before diving into using hashtags, it's important to understand their power and the role they play on social media. Hashtags are words or phrases preceded by the "#" symbol that allow users to categorize their content and make it easier for others to find. When users search or click on a specific hashtag, they're presented with all posts using that tag, enabling them to discover new content and connect with other users interested in the same topic.

Researching Relevant Hashtags

To use hashtags strategically, it's essential to conduct thorough research on those most relevant to your industry, brand, or content topics. Use tools like Instagram's Explore Page, TikTok's Discover Page, or Twitter's Trending Topics to discover which hashtags are popular and relevant to your target audience. Also, try to understand which hashtags your competitors or other influencers in your industry use.

Using a Combination of Popular and Niche Hashtags

When selecting hashtags to use in your posts, it's important to strike a balance between popular and niche hashtags. Popular hashtags have a large volume of use and can help you reach a broad audience but can also be highly competitive. Niche hashtags, on the other hand, have a smaller audience but are less competitive and can help you reach more qualified users interested in your content. Use a combination of both to maximize your post's visibility.

Using Relevant and Specific Hashtags

Avoid using generic or overly broad hashtags that may not be relevant to your content or target audience. Instead, aim to use relevant, specific, and targeted hashtags that accurately describe your content and the topic at hand. This way, you'll attract a more qualified audience and increase the chances of generating meaningful engagement and interactions.

Limiting the Number of Hashtags

Although Instagram allows up to 30 hashtags per post, it's not always necessary to max out this limit. Instead, aim to keep the number of hashtags between 5 and 10 per post and choose the most relevant and effective ones for your content. Too many hashtags can appear spammy and distract from your post's main message, so it's better to focus on quality over quantity.

Incorporating Hashtags into Your Content Strategy

Hashtags should not be seen as a random addition to your posts but rather as an integral part of your social media content strategy. Plan in advance which hashtags you'll use for each post and ensure they align with the themes and goals of your campaign or brand. Also, create custom hashtags for your specific campaigns or events and encourage your followers to use them in their posts.

Monitoring and Analyzing Hashtag Performance

Once you've started using hashtags in your posts, it's important to monitor and analyze their performance to understand which ones are most effective for your audience. Use analytics tools like Instagram Insights, TikTok Analytics, or Twitter Analytics to track reach, impressions, and engagement generated by each hashtag. Based on this data, you can optimize your hashtag strategy and focus on those that yield the best results.

Adapting Your Hashtag Strategy

Finally, remember that hashtag strategy is not static and should be continuously adapted and optimized based on changes in your audience, social media algorithms, and market trends. Experiment with new hashtags, monitor the results, and make any necessary changes to your hashtag strategy based on feedback and results.

Conclusion

Using hashtags strategically is essential for increasing visibility, engagement, and success of your content on social media. Follow the best practices and strategies outlined in this chapter to select the most relevant and effective hashtags for your target audience and to optimize your content strategy on platforms like Instagram, TikTok, and Twitter. Experiment, monitor results, and adapt your hashtag strategy based on feedback and results, and you'll see your presence and influence on social media grow.

*NOTES:*_____

_____

_____

_____

_____

_____

_____

_____

_____

_____

_____

_____

_____

_____

_____

_____

_____

_____

_____

_____

_____

_____

_____

_____

_____

_____

_____

_____

_____

Chapter 6 - Collaborations and Partnerships to Increase Visibility

Introduction

In the realm of social media, collaborations and partnerships have become an effective way to enhance visibility and engagement with one's content. By teaming up with other creators, brands, or influencers, it's possible to expand one's audience, reach new market niches, and create more diverse and engaging content. In this chapter, we'll explore the importance of collaborations and partnerships on platforms like Instagram, YouTube, TikTok, and other social media, providing advice and strategies on how to leverage them to maximize profile visibility.

Understanding the Potential of Collaborations

Collaborations and partnerships offer numerous advantages for creators and brands on social media. Firstly, they enable reaching a broader audience through exposure to each other's audiences. Additionally, collaborations provide an opportunity to create more interesting and engaging content, thanks to the diversity of perspectives and styles of the involved partners. Finally, partnerships can also lead to new revenue opportunities through sponsorships, affiliations, or business agreements with brands and companies.

Identifying Potential Partners

The first step in initiating a successful collaboration is identifying potential partners who align with your brand, values, and target audience. These can be other creators, influencers, brands, or companies operating in your same industry or complementary sectors. Utilize search tools like social media platforms, influencer directories, or collaboration platforms to find the right partners for your strategy.

Creating Engaging Collaboration Proposals

Once potential partners are identified, it's important to create engaging and compelling collaboration proposals that demonstrate the value of the partnership for both involved parties. Clearly outline the collaboration's objectives, the benefits for both parties, agreement details, and mutual expectations. Customize your proposals based on specific partners and strive to create an offer that resonates with their interests and goals.

Building Long-Term Relationships

Successful collaborations often rely on long-term, mutually respectful relationships. Strive to establish authentic and lasting relationships with your partners, based on trust, transparency, and collaboration. Communicate openly and honestly with your partners and endeavor to meet their needs and expectations, just as you expect them to do with you.

Experimenting with Various Forms of Collaboration

There are numerous forms of collaboration to explore on social media. These may include content creation collaborations, sponsorships, affiliations, joint events or promotions, giveaways, account takeovers, and more. Experiment with different forms of collaboration to see which ones work best with your audience and partners, and adjust your strategy accordingly.

Measuring and Evaluating Performance

It's important to monitor and evaluate the performance of your collaborations to understand which ones are most effective in achieving your goals. Use analytics and monitoring tools to track reach, engagement, conversions, and other key metrics associated with your collaborations. Analyze the results obtained and use this information to optimize your future collaborations and partnerships.

Maintaining Open and Continuous Communication

Open and continuous communication is essential for the success of collaborations and partnerships. Ensure to maintain constant dialogue with your partners, sharing updates, feedback, and ideas in a timely and transparent manner. Promptly respond to your partners' questions and requests and work together to address any issues or conflicts that may arise along the way.

Continuously Seeking New Collaboration Opportunities

Collaboration opportunities are endless on social media, so never stop seeking new partners and collaboration opportunities that can help you grow and achieve your goals. Stay open to unexpected collaboration possibilities and strive to maintain a flexible and adaptable approach to the changing needs of the market and your audience.

Conclusion

Collaborations and partnerships are an important strategy for increasing the visibility and engagement of your content on social media. Follow the advice and strategies outlined in this chapter to identify the right partners, create compelling collaboration proposals, and build long-term relationships that lead to mutual success. With a strategic and collaborative approach, collaborations can become a significant lever for growing and expanding your presence on social media.

*NOTES:*_____

Chapter 7 - How to Use Instagram Stories to Engage Your Audience

Introduction

Instagram Stories have become an essential tool for engaging the audience on Instagram. With their temporary and interactive nature, stories offer a unique way to connect with your followers, share creative content, and boost engagement. In this chapter, we'll explore best practices and strategies for using Instagram Stories effectively and engagingly, to increase your profile's visibility and create an active and involved community.

Understanding Instagram Stories Features

Before diving into using Instagram Stories, it's important to familiarize yourself with the various features and tools available. These include temporary photos and videos, text, freehand drawing, stickers, filters, polls, questions, countdowns, and much more. Experiment with different features to create dynamic and engaging stories that capture your followers' attention.

Creating Authentic and Creative Content

Instagram Stories provide a unique opportunity to showcase the authentic and creative side of your brand or personality. Use stories to share behind-the-scenes moments, everyday life, sneak peeks of new products or services, tutorials, tips, and more. Be genuine, transparent, and creative in your content to stimulate your followers' interest and engagement.

Using Stickers and Interactive Features

Stickers and interactive features are a great way to engage the audience and encourage interaction with your Instagram Stories. Use stickers such as polls, questions, quizzes, countdowns, emoji sliders, GIFs, and more to invite your followers to actively participate in your stories. Respond to comments and direct messages from your followers and create a two-way dialogue to foster deeper and more meaningful engagement.

Using Instagram Stories to Promote Content and Offers

Instagram Stories can be effectively used to promote content, offers, and special promotions on your profile. Use stories to share previews of new posts, videos, or blogs on your main feed, or to inform your followers about discounts, sales, or ongoing events. Also, use swipe-up features (if available) to direct your followers directly to external links, such as articles, products, or landing pages.

Planning and Scheduling Instagram Stories

Although Instagram Stories are temporary by nature, it's still possible to plan and schedule them in advance using social media management tools or automation platforms. Plan your stories based on an editorial calendar and specific goals, and use analytics tools to monitor the performance of your stories and make any necessary changes to your content strategy.

Collaborating with Other Creators and Brands

Instagram Stories offer a unique opportunity to collaborate with other creators, influencers, or brands to create joint content and expand your visibility. Organize account takeovers, creative collaborations, joint promotions, or special events on Instagram to engage your partners' audience and expand your own audience. Collaborate with partners who have a similar or complementary audience to maximize the impact of your shared stories.

Analyzing Performance and Optimizing Strategy

It's important to regularly monitor and analyze the performance of your Instagram Stories using built-in analytics tools or third-party platforms. Analyze metrics such as reach, engagement, views, responses, and more to understand which types of content work best with your audience and adjust your strategy accordingly. Experiment with different tactics, formats, and posting frequencies to optimize the performance of your Instagram Stories over time.

Conclusion

Instagram Stories are a powerful tool for engaging the audience on Instagram and creating a deeper and more authentic connection with your followers. Follow the best practices and strategies outlined in this chapter to use Instagram Stories effectively and engagingly, and to maximize the visibility and engagement of your profile on Instagram. Experiment, monitor results, and adapt your content strategy based on feedback and results, and you'll see increased engagement and interaction with your audience on Instagram.

*NOTES:*_____

Chapter 8 - The Importance of Interaction and Engagement

Introduction

In the world of social media, interaction and engagement have become crucial elements for the success of any online presence. Now more than ever, social platforms like Instagram, Facebook, Twitter, and TikTok evaluate not only the quantity but also the quality of interactions between users and content. In this chapter, we will explore the importance of interaction and engagement on social media, examining how these metrics influence visibility, credibility, and audience engagement.

Definition of Interaction and Engagement on Social Media

First and foremost, it's important to clarify what is meant by interaction and engagement on social media. Interaction refers to user actions such as likes, comments, shares, direct messages, and link clicks. Engagement, on the other hand, is a broader measure that takes into account user interactions along with the quality of engagement, such as time spent on content, number of views, and depth of conversations.

Impact of Interaction and Engagement on Visibility

Social platforms use complex algorithms to determine which content to show to users and in what order. One of the key factors considered by these algorithms is the audience's interaction and engagement with the content. Posts with a high rate of interaction tend to be favored by algorithms and shown to a wider audience, thereby increasing the visibility of the profile and its content.

Building Communities and Authentic Connections

Interaction and engagement are fundamental to building communities and authentic connections on social media. When users feel engaged and involved, they are more likely to regularly return to your profile, interact with your content, and share their experiences with other users. This creates a virtuous cycle of engagement that can lead to organic growth of your community.

Building Credibility and Reliability

A high level of interaction and engagement on social media can help build your credibility and reliability in your industry or market niche. When users see others positively engaging with your content, they are more likely to consider you an authority in your field and to trust your opinions, advice, or recommendations. This can lead to collaboration opportunities, partnerships, and long-term monetization.

Active Engagement vs. Passive Engagement

Not all interactions and engagements are equal. It's important to distinguish between active engagement and passive engagement and focus on promoting more meaningful and significant engagement with your audience. Active engagement includes actions such as commenting, sharing, responding to polls or questions, while passive engagement may include simply viewing the content without actively interacting with it.

Strategies to Increase Interaction and Engagement

There are several strategies you can use to increase interaction and engagement from your audience on social media. These include creating engaging and high-quality content, timely response to comments and direct messages, active participation in relevant conversations and communities, use of clear and inviting call-to-action, and collaboration with other creators or brands to expand your audience.

Measuring and Monitoring Interaction and Engagement

It's important to regularly measure and monitor the interaction and engagement of your audience on social media to understand which strategies work best and adapt your strategy accordingly. Use integrated analytics tools or third-party platforms to track metrics such as the number of likes, comments, shares, views, and more. Analyze the data collected to identify trends, patterns, and improvement opportunities for your content strategy.

The Importance of Feedback and Active Listening

Finally, don't forget the importance of feedback and active listening in engaging your audience on social media. Pay attention to comments, reviews, questions, and suggestions from your followers and respond promptly and respectfully. Show appreciation for your followers' feedback and use it to continuously improve your content strategy and approach to communication on social media.

Conclusions

Interaction and engagement are fundamental to the success of any online presence on social media. Invest time and energy in creating engaging content, actively participating in conversations, and carefully listening to your audience's feedback. Use the strategies and tactics described in this chapter to increase interaction and engagement from your audience on social media and create an active, engaged, and loyal community around your profile and content.

*NOTES:*_____

_____

_____

_____

_____

_____

_____

_____

_____

_____

_____

_____

_____

_____

_____

_____

_____

_____

_____

_____

_____

_____

_____

_____

_____

_____

_____

_____

_____

Chapter 9 - Analyzing Results and Adapting Strategy

Introduction

In the world of social media marketing, analyzing results and adapting strategy are crucial for long-term success. Without regular evaluation of performance and the ability to adapt to changes in audience behavior and platform algorithms, it's easy to fall behind and miss out on the opportunity to grow your online presence. In this chapter, we'll explore the importance of result analysis and strategy adaptation to increase followers on Instagram, providing practical tips and guidelines on how to evaluate performance, identify areas for improvement, and optimize your content strategy.

Defining Key Success Metrics

The first step in result analysis is defining key success metrics that will determine the effectiveness of your Instagram growth strategy. These metrics may include the number of new followers acquired, engagement rate (likes, comments, shares), reach, content interaction (link clicks, post saves), website or online shop traffic growth, and more. Ensure to select metrics that are most relevant to your growth goals and regularly measure their progress over time.

Using Integrated and Third-Party Analytics Tools

Instagram offers a range of integrated analytics tools that allow you to monitor your account and content performance. Use tools like Instagram Insights to gain detailed insights into reach, engagement, and audience behavior. Additionally, consider using third-party platforms like Hootsuite, Sprout Social, or Buffer to obtain deeper analysis and advanced monitoring and reporting features.

Monitoring and Evaluating Content Performance

A fundamental part of result analysis is monitoring and evaluating the performance of your content on Instagram. Analyze which types of content generate the most engagement and resonate most with your target audience. Pay attention to themes, styles, formats, and posting times that work best and adapt your content strategy based on this data.

Identifying Trends and Opportunities

In addition to monitoring content performance, it's also important to identify emerging trends and opportunities on Instagram. Keep an eye on what your competitors, influencers in your industry, and broader market trends are doing. Seek to capitalize on these trends and opportunities by creating relevant and timely content that captures your audience's attention and stands out from the crowd.

Collecting and Interpreting Follower Feedback

Your followers' feedback is a valuable resource for evaluating the effectiveness of your Instagram growth strategy. Monitor comments, direct messages, and interactions with your followers to understand what they appreciate about your content and what they would like to see more of. Consider their opinions and suggestions and use them to inform your decisions and adapt your strategy accordingly.

Testing and Experimenting with New Strategies

Result analysis provides valuable insights into what works and what doesn't in your Instagram growth strategy. Use this information to test and experiment with new strategies and tactics aimed at improving your account's performance. Be willing to try out new ideas, formats, and approaches and adapt your strategy based on the results.

Continuously Optimizing Your Strategy

Result analysis and strategy adaptation are not static processes but continuously evolving. Continue to monitor your account's performance on Instagram and adapt your strategy based on changes in audience behavior, market trends, and platform algorithms. Be flexible, responsive, and ready to modify your strategy to maximize effectiveness and achieve meaningful results in the long term.

Measuring and Celebrating Successes

Finally, make sure to measure and celebrate successes achieved through result analysis and strategy adaptation. Recognize and appreciate the progress made in achieving your Instagram growth goals and use these successes as motivation to continue improving and growing. Remember that success on social media takes time, commitment, and consistency, but with the right strategy and approach, you can achieve great results in the long term.

Conclusion

Result analysis and strategy adaptation are essential for the success of your Instagram growth strategy. Follow the tips and guidelines outlined in this chapter to regularly evaluate your account's performance, identify areas for improvement, and optimize your content strategy to maximize effectiveness and achieve meaningful results in the long term. With a systematic and data-driven approach, you can increase followers on Instagram and create a successful online presence that stands out from the competition.

Chapter 10 - Advanced Techniques to Accelerate Instagram Follower Growth

Introduction

In the fast-paced and competitive arena of Instagram, increasing followers is a priority for many creators, influencers, and brands. However, gaining a significant number of followers isn't always easy and requires advanced and innovative strategies. In this chapter, we'll explore advanced techniques to accelerate follower growth on Instagram. We'll analyze advanced strategies, provide concrete examples, and suggest how to effectively implement them to achieve tangible results.

Collaboration and Partnership Strategies

Collaborations and partnerships with other creators or brands can be an effective way to quickly increase followers on Instagram. These partnerships can take various forms, including:

Content creation collaborations: Partner with other creators to create shared content that interests both audiences. For example, a fashion blogger could collaborate with a clothing brand to create a series of style posts.

Shoutout exchanges: Organize shoutout exchanges with other Instagram accounts similar to yours. This can help expose your profile to a new audience interested in your content.

Sponsorship partnerships: Work with brands or companies to create sponsorship partnerships that include promotional posts or giveaways. This can lead to a significant increase in followers due to the additional visibility provided by the brand partner.

Account takeovers: Organize account takeovers with other creators or brands, allowing them to temporarily post on your account to expose your audience to their audience and vice versa.

Effective Use of Hashtags

Hashtags are a powerful tool to increase the visibility of your posts on Instagram and attract new followers. However, using them effectively requires more than just keywords. Here are some advanced techniques to maximize hashtag usage:

Research and use of relevant and popular hashtags: Use research tools like Hashtagify or Trendsmap to identify the most relevant and popular hashtags in your niche.

Use of less competitive hashtags: In addition to popular hashtags, consider using less competitive and more specific hashtags to increase the chances of appearing in the "Top Posts" section.

Mix of broadness hashtags: Use a combination of hashtags of different breadth, including very popular hashtags, niche hashtags, and custom hashtags to reach a variety of audiences.

Regular rotation of hashtags: Avoid using the same hashtags all the time and try to regularly change your selection to maintain audience interest and maximize your exposure.

Creation of Engaging and High-Quality Content

Creating engaging and high-quality content is essential to attract and retain followers on Instagram. Here are some advanced techniques to improve your content:

Use of innovative formats: Experiment with innovative content formats such as 360-degree videos, interactive carousels, slideshow posts, and user-generated content to capture the audience's attention and differentiate yourself from the competition.

Content personalization: Customize your content for your target audience, using language, tone, and visual style that resonate with them and emotionally engage them.

Storytelling usage: Use the power of storytelling to create content that evokes emotions and connections with the audience. Tell authentic and relevant stories that allow followers to feel involved and engaged in your brand or personal narrative.

Trend monitoring: Stay up-to-date with trends and trending topics on Instagram and try to integrate them into your content creatively and relevantly.

Active Engagement with the Audience

Active interaction with the audience is crucial for building a community of loyal and engaged followers. Here are some advanced techniques to actively engage the audience on Instagram:

Timely response to comments and direct messages: Respond promptly to comments and direct messages from your followers to demonstrate your commitment and willingness to interact with them.

Use of polls and questions in Instagram Stories: Use the interactive features of Instagram Stories, such as polls, questions, and quizzes, to actively engage the audience and gather feedback.

Organization of events and contests: Organize events or contests on Instagram that encourage audience engagement and reward active participation.

Encouragement of user sharing: Encourage your followers to share your content and tag their friends in your posts to expand your audience and increase engagement.

Result Analysis and Strategy Adaptation

Finally, result analysis and strategy adaptation are crucial for the long-term success of your Instagram growth strategy. Here's how you can implement this advanced technique:

Constant monitoring of key success metrics: Use analytics tools to regularly monitor key success metrics such as the number of followers, engagement rate, and reach.

Content performance evaluation: Regularly analyze the performance of your content to identify what works and what doesn't with your audience. Look at engagement metrics, comments, shares, and other interactions to understand which types of content generate the most engagement.

Trend and opportunity identification: Recognize and capitalize on emerging trends and opportunities in your industry. Monitor what your competitors are doing and try to capitalize on relevant trends and topics for your audience.

Strategy adaptation based on data: Based on result analysis, adapt your Instagram growth strategy. Modify your content, the hashtags you use, your engagement tactics, and partnerships based on the data you collect. Be flexible and ready to make adjustments to optimize your account's performance.

Testing and experimenting with new ideas: Don't be afraid to experiment with new ideas and approaches to accelerate your Instagram follower growth. Test new types of content, engagement strategies, and partnerships to see what works best with your audience.

Concrete Examples

1. Influencer Collaboration: A sportswear brand collaborates with a fitness influencer to create a series of posts and stories showcasing the product in action during a workout. The influencer shares the content with their audience, leading to a significant increase in followers for the brand.

2. Creative Use of Hashtags: A travel photographer uses a combination of popular and less competitive hashtags in their Instagram posts. This allows them to appear in both the "Top Posts" section for popular hashtags and the "Recent Posts" section for niche hashtags, increasing the visibility of their profile and attracting new followers interested in travel.

3. Creation of Engaging Content: A cosmetics company uses tutorial videos to show how to use their products in creative and innovative ways. These videos are engaging and informative, capturing the audience's attention and encouraging them to follow the account for further tips and inspiration.

4. Active Audience Engagement: A fashion brand organizes a contest on Instagram asking followers to share their photos wearing their products with a specific hashtag. This encourages active audience engagement and generates a large amount of user-generated content that can be shared on the brand's profile.

Conclusion

Accelerating follower growth on Instagram requires a strategic and creative approach. By using advanced techniques such as collaborations, effective hashtag usage, creation of engaging content, active audience engagement, and result analysis, you can quickly increase the number of followers and build a successful online presence on this increasingly important social platform. Experiment with different strategies and tactics, monitor the results, and continually adapt your strategy based on the data you collect. With consistency, commitment, and creativity, you can achieve significant results and establish your position as an influencer or leading brand on Instagram.

*NOTES:*_____

Conclusions

Instagram, one of the most popular social platforms in the world, utilizes a complex algorithm to determine which content is shown to users in their feed. Understanding how this algorithm works is crucial to maximize visibility and engagement on your Instagram profile. In this chapter, we'll delve into how the Instagram algorithm functions, the factors influencing content distribution, and the best practices to optimize your profile and increase visibility on the platform.

Before diving into optimizing your Instagram profile or creating engaging content, it's essential to understand who your target audience is. This means analyzing your current and potential followers, understanding their preferences, interests, and online behaviors. Only by having a deep understanding of your audience can you create targeted content and marketing strategies that resonate with them and engage them meaningfully.

Your Instagram profile is your online storefront and must be optimized to maximize audience appeal and engagement. This entails curating the aesthetic of your profile, using an eye-catching profile picture, a clear and concise bio, and a link to your website or other relevant platforms. Additionally, make sure to use relevant keywords in your bio and carefully select featured content to showcase the best of you and your brand.

Creating engaging and high-quality content is essential to attract and retain followers on Instagram. Invest time and energy into creating photos, videos, and stories that are authentic, relevant, and interesting to your target audience. Experiment with different content formats and styles, and use editing and post-production tools to enhance the visual quality of your posts.

Hashtags are a powerful tool to increase the visibility of your posts on Instagram and reach a wider audience. However, it's important to use hashtags strategically and purposefully. Research the most relevant and popular hashtags in your niche industry and use them sparingly in your posts. Avoid using overly generic or irrelevant hashtags, and be aware of trends and trending hashtags to maximize your exposure.

Collaborations and partnerships with other creators or brands can be an effective way to increase the visibility of your profile on Instagram. Seek collaborations with accounts similar to yours or with brands that share similar values and interests. These partnerships can include shoutout exchanges, collaborations for creating shared content, or sponsorship partnerships that offer additional visibility to your profile.

Instagram Stories offer a unique opportunity to engage your audience in a immediate and authentic way. Use stories to share behind-the-scenes, everyday life moments, previews of new products or services, tutorials, tips, and more. Take advantage of the interactive features of stories, such as polls, questions, quizzes, and countdowns, to stimulate engagement and gather feedback from your followers.

Interaction and engagement are crucial for the success of any profile on Instagram. Respond promptly to comments and direct messages from your followers, actively participate in conversations on the platform, and use the interactive features of stories to engage your audience meaningfully. The more interaction and engagement you generate, the more your profile will be favored by the Instagram algorithm and shown to a wider audience.

Finally, result analysis and strategy adaptation are crucial for the long-term success of your Instagram profile. Regularly monitor key success metrics such as the number of followers, engagement rate, and reach of your content, and adapt your strategy based on the data you collect. Experiment with new ideas and approaches, and continuously strive to improve and optimize the performance of your profile.

To further accelerate the growth of your followers on Instagram, consider using advanced techniques such as collaborations with influencers or brands, participation in contests or events, the use of automation tools to increase the visibility of your profile, and in-depth research and analysis of market trends and audience behavior. Experiment with different strategies and tactics and seek to capitalize on emerging opportunities to maximize the growth of your profile on Instagram.

NOTES:_____

_____
_____
_____
_____
_____
_____
_____
_____
_____
_____
_____
_____
_____
_____
_____
_____
_____
_____
_____
_____
_____
_____
_____
_____
_____
_____
_____
_____

*NOTES:*_____

_____

_____

_____

_____

_____

_____

_____

_____

_____

_____

_____

_____

_____

_____

_____

_____

_____

_____

_____

_____

_____

_____

_____

_____

_____

_____

_____

_____

_____

*NOTES:*_____